Saturn

by
Christine Taylor-Butler

Children's Press
An Imprint of Scholastic Inc.
New York Toronto London Auckland Sydney
Mexico City New Delhi Hong Kong
Danbury, Connecticut

These content vocabulary word builders
are for grades 1–2.

Consultant: Michelle Yehling, Astronomy Education Consultant

Photo Credits:

Photographs © 2008: Corbis Images/Jim Zuckerman: 5 bottom right, 16; Finley Holiday Film: back cover; Getty Images/Antonio M. Rosario/The Image Bank: 4 bottom right, 13; NASA: 5 bottom left, 5 top right (Jet Propulsion Lab Photo), 9, 11, 17 (JPL/Space Science Institute), cover, 1, 4 bottom left, 7, 19, 23 right; Photo Researchers, NY: 2, 4 top, 15 (Lynette Cook/SPL); PhotoDisc/Getty Images via SODA: 23 left.

Illustration Credit:

Illustration pages 5 top left, 20–21 by Greg Harris

Book Design: Simonsays Design!
Book Production: The Design Lab

Library of Congress Cataloging-in-Publication Data
Taylor-Butler, Christine.
Saturn / by Christine Taylor-Butler.—Updated ed.
    p. cm.—(Scholastic news nonfiction readers)
Includes bibliographical references and index.
ISBN-13: 978-0-531-14752-8 (lib. bdg.)   978-0-531-14767-2 (pbk.)
ISBN-10: 0-531-14752-5 (lib.bdg.)   0-531-14767-3 (pbk.)
1. Saturn (Planet)—Juvenile literature. I. Title.
QB671.T235 2007
523.46—dc22   2006102773

Published by Children's Press, an imprint of Scholastic Inc.
Published simultaneously in Canada. Printed in the United States of America. 44

1 2 3 4 5 6 7 8 9 10 R 17 16 15 14 13 12 11 10 09 08

CONTENTS

WORD HUNT

Look for these words as you read. They will be in **bold**.

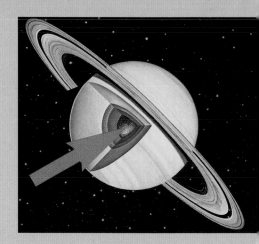

core
(kor)

Saturn
(**sat**-urn)

solar system
(**soh**-lur **siss**-tuhm)

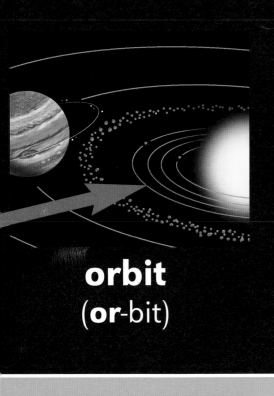

orbit
(**or**-bit)

rings
(ringz)

Titan
(**tie**-tuhn)

tornado
(tor-**nay**-doh)

Saturn!

Saturn has **rings**.

The rings **orbit**, or travel around, the planet.

There is ice in Saturn's rings.

Can you skate on Saturn's rings? No.

The rings are not one solid piece. There is ice but also dust, rock, and empty space, too.

Other planets also have rings.

But Saturn has the most rings.

Scientists think there are 10,000 rings or more around Saturn.

Saturn's rings are very wide and very flat.

There are at least 56 moons that orbit Saturn.

The largest moon is **Titan**.

It has an atmosphere and clouds. An atmosphere is the gas that surrounds an object in space.

Titan was discovered in 1655.

Saturn is the sixth planet from the Sun.

Saturn is the second largest planet in the **solar system**.

All the planets in the solar system orbit the Sun.

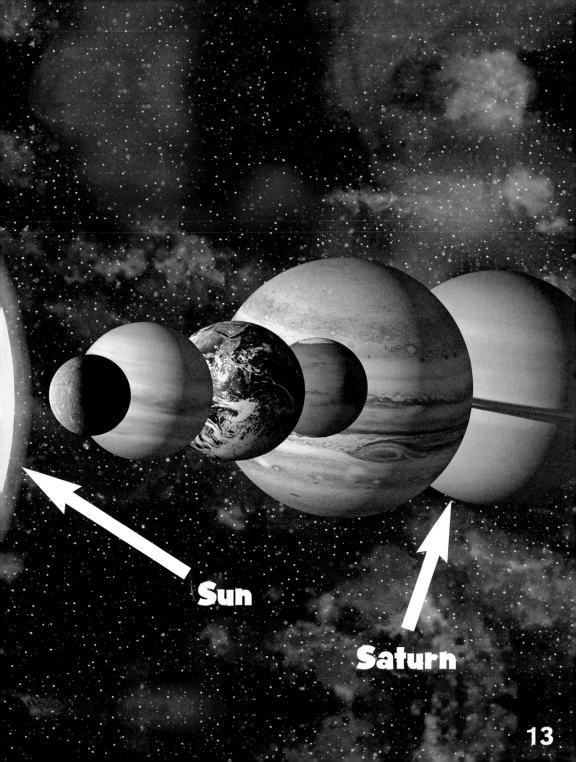

Sun

Saturn

13

Saturn is a giant ball of gas.

Deep inside the planet the gas becomes a hot liquid.

At the very middle of the planet is the **core**. The core is made mostly of rock.

core

On Saturn, the wind blows very fast.

Sometimes the wind blows 1,100 miles per hour.

That is more than five times faster than the winds inside a **tornado** on Earth!

tornado

Saturn is very big, but it is one of the lightest planets.

One of the gases it is made of is helium.

That's the gas that makes balloons float!

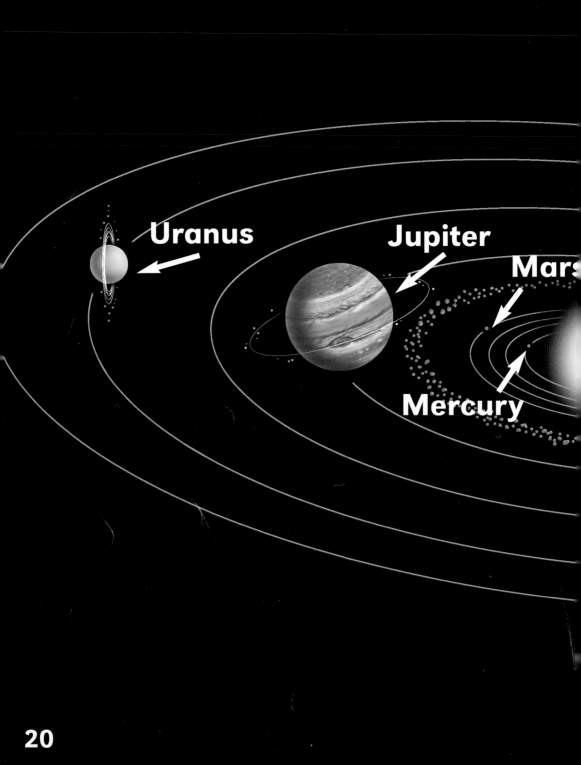

Uranus

Jupiter

Mars

Mercury

SATURN

IN OUR SOLAR SYSTEM

Sun

Venus

Saturn

Earth

Neptune

YOUR NEW WORDS

core (kor) the inside of an object

orbit (**or**-bit) to travel around a planet or the Sun

rings (ringz) bands of rocks, dust, and ice that circle a planet

Saturn (**sat**-urn) a planet named after the Roman god of the harvest

solar system (**soh**-lur **siss**-tuhm) the group of planets, moons, and other things that travel around the Sun

Titan (**tie**-tuhn) the largest moon of Saturn

tornado (tor-**nay**-doh) a funnel-shaped windstorm

Earth and Saturn

A year is how long it takes a planet to go around the Sun.

**1 Earth year
=365 days**

**1 Saturn year
=10,756 Earth days**

A day is how long it takes a planet to turn one time.

**1 Earth day
= 24 hours**

**1 Saturn day
= 11 Earth hours**

A moon is a big rock that circles a planet.

**Earth has
1 moon.**

**Saturn has 56
moons with more
being found all
the time.**

You can fit about 764
Earths inside of Saturn.

INDEX

FIND OUT MORE

Book:

Burnham, Robert. *Children's Atlas of the Universe.* Pleasantville, NY: Reader's Digest Children's Publishing, Inc., 2000.

Web site:

Solar System Exploration
http://sse.jpl.nasa.gov/planets

MEET THE AUTHOR

Christine Taylor-Butler is the author of more than twenty books for children. She holds a degree in Engineering from M.I.T. She lives in Kansas City with her family, where they have a telescope for searching the skies.